The Little Book of BIG MOON BLESSINGS

An Inspirational Journal

USA TODAY BESTSELLING AUTHOR
MISTY EVANS

The Little Book of Big Moon Blessings
An Inspirational Journal
©2022 Misty Evans.
All Rights Reserved.
ISBN: 978-1-948686-67-9

Hello, Beautiful Soul!

The moon brings many blessings as it cycles through its waxing and waning evolutions. Since the beginning of time, the moon has been associated with the feminine and our emotions. The beauty of it has captured mankind's imagination and inspired our lives.

Scientists have learned a great deal about our solar system from the moon. It influences our tides, both those in nature and those within us, due to the fact our bodies are sixty percent water. Migration, navigation, and reproductive cycles are affected by it, and the very axis of our planet is stabilized by it.

The moon is the Earth's only natural satellite, and energetically, we can use it as a guiding force to understand the cycles of our lives and empower our dreams. The moon's cooling rays, a reflection of the sun on its surface, offer us a soothing and nurturing light. The waning and waxing energies can power up manifestation, health, and dreamwork. The fact it has been present in the night sky since the beginning of our world gives us a link to our ancestors. They, too, gazed up at it, slept under it, and counted the seasons by it.

How can the moon's energy make life easier and healthier? The "magic" of the moon is energy, its gravitational pull. Just like it creates the tides, its pull can deepen our intuition and cause our emotions to surface. We can use it to understand ourselves on a more intuitive level, learn to receive as much as we give, connect to ancient wisdom, and live more in tune with nature. Working with circadian rhythms and lunar rhythms makes life flow more easily. Humans are the only species that move out of alignment with nature and the seasons.

You can harness the power of the moon by harmonizing with its phases. By timing daily events, spiritual practices, and routines in sync with the energy of its cycles, the moon can have a significant positive impact on your state of mind, as well as your body.

How to Use the Moon's Phases To Empower You

The Moon is a guiding light in the night sky that cycles from the new or 'dark' moon to the full moon, repeating each month. A lunar month is the time it takes the moon to go from new (when it is aligned with the sun) back to new again (this is after it has made one complete orbit of the earth, which takes on average 29 days, 12 hours and 44 minutes).

A **new moon** is the beginning of the lunar cycle and lasts three days. This is like a mini New Year's Day each month – a time of renewed energy and thinking about of what you wish to accomplish in the coming few weeks or months. It's a time of possibility!

Visualize what you wish for, write down new moon wishes, and dream big. Blessings will flow when you allow yourself to believe anything is possible and don't let limiting or negative thoughts weigh you down.

While this time is not action-oriented, the new moon can bring clarity and insight into what you really desire and what step(s) to take to make it a reality.

The **waxing moon** comes next and the blessing of this phase is its creative and productive power. Your energy levels increase. Motivation is activated. Like those first days of the New Year, kicking off resolutions, ditching bad habits, and taking steps toward your goal, even baby ones, are easier to do. The trick here is not to overdo or allow doubts and negative self-talk to sabotage you.

Your intuition, aka internal guidance system, will be highly active at this time, so be sure to tune in and listen to it.

Note: There are stages when a goal needs more time or we may need to take a different path to get to it. This, too, can create stress or impatience. Like the tides, go with it, and know that you're learning and growing, like the increasing reflection of light on the moon.

The **full moon** arrives bearing gifts—dreams come to fruition, goals are accomplished. It arrives fourteen to fifteen days after the new moon and the energy peaks now. The spotlight is on what you've accomplished, and also on what you may need to release: limiting beliefs, outdated habits, things that aren't working. In their place, the moon's glow spotlights what you may need to create a happier, healthier you.

As the light of the moon begins to recede once again during the **waning moon**, your energy may do the same. If your ideas and goals didn't work out in the past few weeks, remember not to give up. The blessing of this cycle narrows the light to refocus on what did work.

This is the time for insight and refining your actions, and also for rest. It's a good time to offer gratitude to the universe for all you have, even if your dream hasn't materialized yet. Nurture yourself, release what isn't working, and communicate with yourself and others, offering and getting the support you need to try again.

January

Moon Cycle:
New Moon

New Moon Questions

What goal do I want to accomplish this month?

What emotions, out dated beliefs or negative thought patterns do I want to release?

January

Moon Cycle:
New Moon

What new belief am I embracing?

What does my heart truly desire?

January

**Moon Cycle:
New Moon**

What does my soul need to move forward?

When I imagine my dreams and desires coming true, what emotions do I feel?

January

**Moon Cycle:
New Moon**

New Moon Wishes

Write or draw your new moon wishes in the space below.

January

Moon Cycle:
New Moon

New Moon Tarot Spread

Date:

Deck:

Questions to ask:

What does the energy of the new moon have in store for me?

What do I need to clear to make way for the new?

What seed am I planting?

What knowledge do I need to make it grow?

What is the outcome?

New Moon free write

New Moon free write

New Moon free write

New Moon free write

**Moon Cycle:
Full Moon**

Full Moon Questions

How did abundance show up in my life since the new moon?

Even if I haven't yet manifested my goal, in what ways am I exactly where I'm meant to be in this moment?

**Moon Cycle:
Full Moon**

What have I manifested during this cycle?

What signs and synchronicities have shown up for me since the new moon?

**Moon Cycle:
Full Moon**

What about this moon makes me grateful?

What's one of my favorite memories from the past month?

**Moon Cycle:
Full Moon**

What is a positive affirmation that I need to hear in this moment?

**Moon Cycle:
Full Moon**

Full Moon Tarot Spread

**Date:
Deck:**

Questions to ask:

What is being illuminated/ needs to be known under the full moon?

What do I need to let go of?

What energy do I need to call in?

What should I focus on now?

 # Full Moon free write

Full Moon free write

 Full Moon free write

 # Full Moon free write

February

Moon Cycle:
New Moon

New Moon Questions

What goal do I want to accomplish this month?

What emotions, out dated beliefs or negative thought patterns do I want to release?

February

Moon Cycle:
New Moon

What new belief am I embracing?

What does my heart truly desire?

February

Moon Cycle:
New Moon

What does my soul need to move forward?

When I imagine my dreams and desires coming true, what emotions do I feel?

February

**Moon Cycle:
New Moon**

New Moon Wishes

Write or draw your new moon wishes in the space below.

February

Moon Cycle:
New Moon

New Moon Tarot Spread

Date:

Deck:

Questions to ask:

What does the energy of the new moon have in store for me?

What do I need to clear to make way for the new?

What seed am I planting?

What knowledge do I need to make it grow?

What is the outcome?

New Moon free write

New Moon free write

New Moon free write

New Moon free write

New Moon free write

**Moon Cycle:
Full Moon**

Full Moon Questions

How did abundance show up in my life since the new moon?

Even if I haven't yet manifested my goal, in what ways am I exactly where I'm meant to be in this moment?

**Moon Cycle:
Full Moon**

What have I manifested during this cycle?

What signs and synchronicities have shown up for me since the new moon?

**Moon Cycle:
Full Moon**

Full Moon Questions

What about this moon makes me grateful?

What's one of my favorite memories from the past month?

**Moon Cycle:
Full Moon**

What is a positive affirmation that I need to hear in this moment?

**Moon Cycle:
Full Moon**

Full Moon Tarot Spread

**Date:
Deck:**

Questions to ask:

What is being illuminated/ needs to be known under the full moon?

What do I need to let go of?

What energy do I need to call in?

What should I focus on now?

# Full Moon free write

Full Moon free write

# Full Moon free write

# Full Moon free write

March

Moon Cycle:
New Moon

New Moon Questions

What goal do I want to accomplish this month?

What emotions, outdated beliefs, or negative thought patterns do I want to release?

March

Moon Cycle:
New Moon

What new belief am I embracing?

What does my heart truly desire?

March

**Moon Cycle:
New Moon**

What does my soul need to move forward?

When I imagine my dreams and desires coming true, what emotions do I feel?

March

**Moon Cycle:
New Moon**

New Moon Wishes

Write or draw your new moon wishes in the space below.

March

Moon Cycle:
New Moon

New Moon Tarot Spread

Date:

Deck:

Questions to ask:

What does the energy of the new moon have in store for me?

What do I need to clear to make way for the new?

What seed and my planting?

What knowledge do I need to make it grow?

What is the outcome?

New Moon free write

New Moon free write

New Moon free write

New Moon free write

**Moon Cycle:
Full Moon**

Full Moon Questions

How did abundance show up in my life since the new moon?

Even if I haven't yet manifested my goal, in what ways am I exactly where I'm meant to be in this moment?

**Moon Cycle:
Full Moon**

What have I manifested during this cycle?

What signs and synchronicities have shown up for me since the new moon?

**Moon Cycle:
Full Moon**

What about this moon makes me grateful?

What's one of my favorite memories from the past month?

**Moon Cycle:
Full Moon**

What is a positive affirmation that I need to hear in this moment?

**Moon Cycle:
Full Moon**

Full Moon Tarot Spread

**Date:
Deck:**

Questions to ask:

What is being illuminated/ needs to be known under the full moon?

What do I need to let go of?

What energy do I need to call in?

What should I focus on now?

Full Moon free write

Full Moon free write

Full Moon free write

Full Moon free write

April

Moon Cycle:
New Moon:

New Moon Questions

What goal do I want to accomplish this month?

What emotions, out dated beliefs or negative thought patterns do I want to release?

April

Moon Cycle:
New Moon:

What new belief am I embracing?

What does my heart truly desire?

April

Moon Cycle:
New Moon:

What does my soul need to move forward?

When I imagine my dreams and desires coming true, what emotions do I feel?

April

Moon Cycle:
New Moon

New Moon Wishes

Write or draw your new moon wishes in the space below.

April

Moon Cycle:
New Moon

New Moon Tarot Spread

Date:

Deck:

Questions to ask:

What does the energy of the new moon have in store for me?

What do I need to clear to make way for the new?

What seed and my planting?

What knowledge do I need to make it grow?

What is the outcome?

New Moon free write

New Moon free write

New Moon free write

New Moon free write

New Moon free write

**Moon Cycle:
Full Moon**

Full Moon Questions

How did abundance show up in my life since the new moon?

Even if I haven't yet manifested my goal, in what ways am I exactly where I'm meant to be in this moment?

**Moon Cycle:
Full Moon**

Full Moon Questions

What have I manifested during this cycle?

What signs and synchronicities have shown up for me since the new moon?

**Moon Cycle:
Full Moon**

What about this moon makes me grateful?

What's one of my favorite memories from the past month?

**Moon Cycle:
Full Moon**

What is a positive affirmation that I need to hear in this moment?

**Moon Cycle:
Full Moon**

Full Moon Tarot Spread

**Date:
Deck:**

Questions to ask:

What is being illuminated/ needs to be known under the full moon?

What do I need to let go of?

What energy do I need to call in?

What should I focus on now?

Full Moon free write

Full Moon free write

Full Moon free write

Full Moon free write

May

Moon Cycle:
New Moon

New Moon Questions

What goal do I want to accomplish this month?

What emotions, out dated beliefs or negative thought patterns do I want to release?

May

**Moon Cycle:
New Moon**

What new belief am I embracing?

What does my heart truly desire?

May

Moon Cycle:
New Moon

What does my soul need to move forward?

When I imagine my dreams and desires coming true, what emotions do I feel?

May

**Moon Cycle:
New Moon**

New Moon Wishes

Write or draw your new moon wishes in the space below.

May

Moon Cycle:
New Moon

New Moon Tarot Spread

Date:

Deck:

Questions to ask:

What does the energy of the new moon have in store for me?

What do I need to clear to make way for the new?

What seed and my planting?

What knowledge do I need to make it grow?

What is the outcome?

New Moon free write

New Moon free write

New Moon free write

New Moon free write

**Moon Cycle:
Full Moon**

Full Moon Questions

How did abundance show up in my life since the new moon?

Even if I haven't yet manifested my goal, in what ways am I exactly where I'm meant to be in this moment?

**Moon Cycle:
Full Moon**

What have I manifested during this cycle?

What signs and synchronicities have shown up for me since the new moon?

**Moon Cycle:
Full Moon**

What about this moon makes me grateful?

What's one of my favorite memories from the past month?

**Moon Cycle:
Full Moon**

What is a positive affirmation that I need to hear in this moment?

**Moon Cycle:
Full Moon**

Full Moon Tarot Spread

**Date:
Deck:**

Questions to ask:

What is being illuminated/ needs to be known under the full moon?

What do I need to let go of?

What energy do I need to call in?

What should I focus on now?

Full Moon free write

# Full Moon free write

# Full Moon free write

Full Moon free write

June

Moon Cycle:
New Moon

New Moon Questions

What goal do I want to accomplish this month?

What emotions, out dated beliefs or negative thought patterns do I want to release?

June

**Moon Cycle:
New Moon**

What new belief am I embracing?

What does my heart truly desire?

June

Moon Cycle:
New Moon

What does my soul need to move forward?

When I imagine my dreams and desires coming true, what emotions do I feel?

June

**Moon Cycle:
New Moon**

New Moon Wishes

Write or draw your new moon wishes in the space below.

June

Moon Cycle:
New Moon

New Moon Tarot Spread

Date:

Deck:

Questions to ask:

What does the energy of the new moon have in store for me?

What do I need to clear to make way for the new?

What seed and my planting?

What knowledge do I need to make it grow?

What is the outcome?

New Moon free write

New Moon free write

New Moon free write

New Moon free write

**Moon Cycle:
Full Moon**

Full Moon Questions

How did abundance show up in my life since the new moon?

Even if I haven't yet manifested my goal, in what ways am I exactly where I'm meant to be in this moment?

**Moon Cycle:
Full Moon**

What have I manifested during this cycle?

What signs and synchronicities have shown up for me since the new moon?

**Moon Cycle:
Full Moon**

What about this moon makes me grateful?

What's one of my favorite memories from the past month?

**Moon Cycle:
Full Moon**

Full Moon Questions

What is a positive affirmation that I need to hear in this moment?

**Moon Cycle:
Full Moon**

Full Moon Tarot Spread

**Date:
Deck:**

Questions to ask:

What is being illuminated/ needs to be known under the full moon?

What do I need to let go of?

What energy do I need to call in?

What should I focus on now?

Full Moon free write

Full Moon free write

Full Moon free write

 # Full Moon free write

July

Moon Cycle:
New Moon

New Moon Questions

What goal do I want to accomplish this month?

What emotions, out dated beliefs or negative thought patterns do I want to release?

July

**Moon Cycle:
New Moon**

What new belief am I embracing?

What does my heart truly desire?

July

Moon Cycle:
New Moon

What does my soul need to move forward?

When I imagine my dreams and desires coming true, what emotions do I feel?

July

**Moon Cycle:
New Moon**

New Moon Wishes

Write or draw your new moon wishes in the space below.

July

Moon Cycle:
New Moon

New Moon Tarot Spread

Date:

Deck:

Questions to ask:

What does the energy of the new moon have in store for me?

What do I need to clear to make way for the new?

What seed and my planting?

What knowledge do I need to make it grow?

What is the outcome?

New Moon free write

New Moon free write

New Moon free write

New Moon free write

**Moon Cycle:
Full Moon**

Full Moon Questions

How did abundance show up in my life since the new moon?

Even if I haven't yet manifested my goal, in what ways am I exactly where I'm meant to be in this moment?

**Moon Cycle:
Full Moon**

What have I manifested during this cycle?

What signs and synchronicities have shown up for me since the new moon?

**Moon Cycle:
Full Moon**

What about this moon makes me grateful?

What's one of my favorite memories from the past month?

**Moon Cycle:
Full Moon**

What is a positive affirmation that I need to hear in this moment?

**Moon Cycle:
Full Moon**

Full Moon Tarot Spread

**Date:
Deck:**

Questions to ask:

What is being illuminated/ needs to be known under the full moon?

What do I need to let go of?

What energy do I need to call in?

What should I focus on now?

Full Moon free write

Full Moon free write

# Full Moon free write

 # Full Moon free write

August

Moon Cycle:
New Moon:

New Moon Questions

What goal do I want to accomplish this month?

What emotions, out dated beliefs or negative thought patterns do I want to release?

August

Moon Cycle:
New Moon

What new belief am I embracing?

What does my heart truly desire?

August

Moon Cycle:
New Moon

What does my soul need to move forward?

When I imagine my dreams and desires coming true, what emotions do I feel?

August

Moon Cycle:
New Moon

Write or draw your new moon wishes in the space below.

August

Moon Cycle:
New Moon:

New Moon Tarot Spread

Date:

Deck:

Questions to ask:

What does the energy of the new moon have in store for me?

What do I need to clear to make way for the new?

What seed and my planting?

What knowledge do I need to make it grow?

What is the outcome?

New Moon free write

New Moon free write

New Moon free write

New Moon free write

**Moon Cycle:
Full Moon**

Full Moon Questions

How did abundance show up in my life since the new moon?

Even if I haven't yet manifested my goal, in what ways am I exactly where I'm meant to be in this moment?

**Moon Cycle:
Full Moon**

What have I manifested during this cycle?

What signs and synchronicities have shown up for me since the new moon?

**Moon Cycle:
Full Moon**

What about this moon makes me grateful?

What's one of my favorite memories from the past month?

**Moon Cycle:
Full Moon**

What is a positive affirmation that I need to hear in this moment?

**Moon Cycle:
Full Moon**

Full Moon Tarot Spread

**Date:
Deck:**

Questions to ask:

What is being illuminated/ needs to be known under the full moon?

What do I need to let go of?

What energy do I need to call in?

What should I focus on now?

# Full Moon free write

Full Moon free write

Full Moon free write

Full Moon free write

September

Moon Cycle:
New Moon

New Moon Questions

What goal do I want to accomplish this month?

What emotions, out dated beliefs or negative thought patterns do I want to release?

September

Moon Cycle:
New Moon

What new belief am I embracing?

What does my heart truly desire?

September

**Moon Cycle:
New Moon**

What does my soul need to move forward?

When I imagine my dreams and desires coming true, what emotions do I feel?

September

**Moon Cycle:
New Moon**

New Moon Wishes

Write or draw your new moon wishes in the space below.

September

Moon Cycle:
New Moon:

New Moon Tarot Spread

Date:

Deck:

Questions to ask:

What does the energy of the new moon have in store for me?

What do I need to clear to make way for the new?

What seed and my planting?

What knowledge do I need to make it grow?

What is the outcome?

New Moon free write

New Moon free write

New Moon free write

New Moon free write

**Moon Cycle:
Full Moon**

Full Moon Questions

How did abundance show up in my life since the new moon?

Even if I haven't yet manifested my goal, in what ways am I exactly where I'm meant to be in this moment?

**Moon Cycle:
Full Moon**

What have I manifested during this cycle?

What signs and synchronicities have shown up for me since the new moon?

**Moon Cycle:
Full Moon**

What about this moon makes me grateful?

What's one of my favorite memories from the past month?

**Moon Cycle:
Full Moon**

What is a positive affirmation that I need to hear in this moment?

Moon Cycle:
Full Moon

Full Moon Tarot Spread

Date:
Deck:

Questions to ask:

What is being illuminated/ needs to be known under the full moon?

What do I need to let go of?

What energy do I need to call in?

What should I focus on now?

Full Moon free write

Full Moon free write

Full Moon free write

Full Moon free write

October

Moon Cycle:
New Moon

New Moon Questions

What goal do I want to accomplish this month?

What emotions, out dated beliefs or negative thought patterns do I want to release?

October

**Moon Cycle:
New Moon**

What new belief am I embracing?

What does my heart truly desire?

October

Moon Cycle:
New Moon

What does my soul need to move forward?

When I imagine my dreams and desires coming true, what emotions do I feel?

October

**Moon Cycle:
New Moon**

New Moon Wishes

Write or draw your new moon wishes in the space below.

October

Moon Cycle:
New Moon

New Moon Tarot Spread

Date:

Deck:

Questions to ask:

What does the energy of the new moon have in store for me?

What do I need to clear to make way for the new?

What seed and my planting?

What knowledge do I need to make it grow?

What is the outcome?

New Moon free write

New Moon free write

New Moon free write

New Moon free write

**Moon Cycle:
Full Moon**

Full Moon Questions

How did abundance show up in my life since the new moon?

Even if I haven't yet manifested my goal, in what ways am I exactly where I'm meant to be in this moment?

**Moon Cycle:
Full Moon**

What have I manifested during this cycle?

What signs and synchronicities have shown up for me since the new moon?

**Moon Cycle:
Full Moon**

What about this moon makes me grateful?

What's one of my favorite memories from the past month?

**Moon Cycle:
Full Moon**

Full Moon Questions

What is a positive affirmation that I need to hear in this moment?

Moon Cycle:
Full Moon

Full Moon Tarot Spread

Date:
Deck:

Questions to ask:

What is being illuminated/ needs to be known under the full moon?

What do I need to let go of?

What energy do I need to call in?

What should I focus on now?

Full Moon free write

Full Moon free write

Full Moon free write

Full Moon free write

November

Moon Cycle:
New Moon

New Moon Questions

What goal do I want to accomplish this month?

What emotions, out dated beliefs or negative thought patterns do I want to release?

November

**Moon Cycle:
New Moon**

What new belief am I embracing?

What does my heart truly desire?

November

Moon Cycle:
New Moon

What does my soul need to move forward?

When I imagine my dreams and desires coming true, what emotions do I feel?

November

**Moon Cycle:
New Moon**

New Moon Wishes

Write or draw your new moon wishes in the space below.

November

Moon Cycle:
New Moon

New Moon Tarot Spread

Date:

Deck:

Questions to ask:

What does the energy of the new moon have in store for me?

What do I need to clear to make way for the new?

What seed and my planting?

**What knowledge do I need to make it grow?
What is the outcome?**

New Moon free write

New Moon free write

New Moon free write

New Moon free write

**Moon Cycle:
Full Moon**

Full Moon Questions

How did abundance show up in my life since the new moon?

Even if I haven't yet manifested my goal, in what ways am I exactly where I'm meant to be in this moment?

**Moon Cycle:
Full Moon**

What have I manifested during this cycle?

What signs and synchronicities have shown up for me since the new moon?

**Moon Cycle:
Full Moon**

What about this moon makes me grateful?

What's one of my favorite memories from the past month?

**Moon Cycle:
Full Moon**

What is a positive affirmation that I need to hear in this moment?

**Moon Cycle:
Full Moon**

Full Moon Tarot Spread

**Date:
Deck:**

Questions to ask:

What is being illuminated/ needs to be known under the full moon?

What do I need to let go of?

What energy do I need to call in?

What should I focus on now?

Full Moon free write

Full Moon free write

Full Moon free write

Full Moon free write

December

Moon Cycle:
New Moon

New Moon Questions

What goal do I want to accomplish this month?

What emotions, out dated beliefs or negative thought patterns do I want to release?

December

**Moon Cycle:
New Moon**

What new belief am I embracing?

What does my heart truly desire?

December

Moon Cycle:
New Moon

What does my soul need to move forward?

When I imagine my dreams and desires coming true, what emotions do I feel?

December

**Moon Cycle:
New Moon**

New Moon Wishes

Write or draw your new moon wishes in the space below.

December

Moon Cycle:
New Moon:

New Moon Tarot Spread

Date:

Deck:

Questions to ask:

What does the energy of the new moon have in store for me?

What do I need to clear to make way for the new?

What seed and my planting?

What knowledge do I need to make it grow?

What is the outcome?

New Moon free write

# New Moon free write

New Moon free write

New Moon free write

New Moon free write

**Moon Cycle:
Full Moon**

Full Moon Questions

How did abundance show up in my life since the new moon?

Even if I haven't yet manifested my goal, in what ways am I exactly where I'm meant to be in this moment?

**Moon Cycle:
Full Moon**

What have I manifested during this cycle?

What signs and synchronicities have shown up for me since the new moon?

**Moon Cycle:
Full Moon**

What about this moon makes me grateful?

What's one of my favorite memories from the past month?

**Moon Cycle:
Full Moon**

What is a positive affirmation that I need to hear in this moment?

**Moon Cycle:
Full Moon**

Full Moon Tarot Spread

**Date:
Deck:**

Questions to ask:

What is being illuminated/ needs to be known under the full moon?

What do I need to let go of?

What energy do I need to call in?

What should I focus on now?

Full Moon free write

Full Moon free write

Full Moon free write

Full Moon free write

BONUS INFO

Eclipses And How To Work With This Energy

Eclipses deal with shadow energy and truth. Secrets that others are keeping from you may be revealed. Secrets that you're keeping from others (or yourself) may also be revealed. It's a good time to be honest before the Universe forces you to.

Many energy workers believe you should not clean or charge crystals, or anything else, during an eclipse. I believe eclipse energy can be effective to work with if you are trying to bring about change, wipe out past programming, and/or start over on a project or soul journey.

It's also a good time for you to relax and reflect. If you want to work with shadow energy – which can be very enlightening: pick a crystal and program it with eclipse energy during the new moon to help you understand yourself better. Then at the full moon, you can release that shadow energy and be done with it.

Because of the chaos of eclipses, effective crystals to work with include Moldavite, Tektite, and Labradorite. I also find heavy metals, such as gold, copper, and pyrite be grounding and protective during this time, and they keep prosperity and abundance flowing into our lives when we may feel a bit unsupported.

To help strengthen and protect your third eye and psychic abilities, I recommend Amethyst and Carnelian.

Of course, any time we're dealing with the sun and the moon, Sunstone and Moonstone are great choices as well.

Refrain from making moon water under an eclipse.

Crystals Associated With The Moon

Crystals are earth energy in a sweet package. Like the moon above us, they've been around since the world began and have been here for every cycle, every season. Some are directly associated with the moon, such as selenite (named after the goddess Selene which means "moon"), moonstone (no surprise with this one), and labradorite (a stone of magic and mystery). Here are a few more that also have ties to our closest celestial body:

Clear quartz – the perfect crystal to capture the light in any setting and magnify it.

Pearl - Pearls have long been connected with the moon and are traditionally associated with Monday ("Moon's Day"). Pearl is also associated with the ancient Roman moon goddess Luna.

Lapis Lazuli – also called "the stone of Heaven" since it is reminiscent of a night sky filled with shiny stars.

Aquamarine and blue calcite – these pair well with the moon because they are connected to the water element

How To Clear And Charge Crystals At Full Moon

Moonlight can clear and charge crystals. A new moon is about beginnings and offers the perfect time to clear a crystal and charge it with a new intention for the coming month.

A full moon is about bringing things to fruition. It's effective for releasing anything that doesn't serve you. The silvery moonbeams clear negativity from the stone and infuse it with nurturing light.

How To Make Moon Water

Tap into the energy of the moon by charging water in the moonlight. Since the moon already influences the Earth's tides, we know it has a natural affinity to the element. When you add your intention, you boost the properties of the water and the moon's energy, creating a tool you can use to do any of the following:

- Bathe in it to soothe the body and improve skin.
- Drink it to energize health.
- Cleanse your home with it to get rid of negative energies.
- Water your plants with it to help them grow.

Instructions: Gather a glass jar or container, such as a mason jar or other clear glass cup. I suggest using something with a lid to keep out unwanted insects and other things who might want to take a dip in it.

Fill it with water from the tap, from a bottle, from a river... just make sure it's safe to drink if you plan on doing so.

Create a label to date the moon water and note the sign and phase the moon is in if you wish.

Water-safe, tumbled (never use raw), crystals such as any listed above.

Add herbs, like mugwort (ruled by the moon), lavender (for relaxation and healing), rosemary (for protection), or sweetgrass (for positive energy) if you feel moved to do so
Set your intention

Charge under a full moon for best results. Enjoy!

Goddesses Associated With The Moon

Lunar deities are found in all ancient religions. The moon represents the Divine Feminine and the watery world of emotions, and working with the lunar goddesses is extremely empowering. You never have to feel alone or lost with these strong and protective goddesses by your side.

Luna – goddess in heaven and of the full moon. Her Greek counterpart is Selene.
Diana – goddess on earth and of the halfmoon. Her Greek counterpart is Artemis.
Hecate (or Hekate) – goddess in the underworld and of the dark moon.

Here are more from various cultures around the world:

Amesemi –Egyptian/Sudan
Cerridwen – Celtic
Hanwi Sioux – Native American Sioux
Heng-O or Ch'ang-O – China
IxChel – Maya
Ilargi – Basque (Spain)
Lona – Hawaiin/Polynesian
Mama Killa or Quilla – Inca
Yemaya – African

I hope you've enjoyed this little book of big moon blessings. Learning about the moon is just the beginning. Dig deeper into astrology and discover what sign your moon was in at your birth, as well as what phase, to unveil more about yourself. Feel empowered by the lunar energies that are always available and at your fingertips to enlighten your life!

Moon blessings on you and yours,

Misty
crystalswithmisty@gmail.com

ABOUT MISTY EVANS

Energy healer, psychic, and shaman, Misty loves working with people on a soul level. Fascinated with past lives, she uses astrology, numerology, spirit guides, as well as good old common sense and her business acumen, to assist clients with resolving energy blocks and discovering their soul's purpose.

Before discovering her own life purpose, she went the traditional route and got a BA in Business, studied marketing and psychology, and thought about becoming a college professor. The Universe intervened and she ended up writing fiction. She is a USA TODAY bestselling author under both of her pen names, and runs her own publishing company.

Misty is a Crystal Reiki Master/Teacher, Usui Traditional Reiki Master, registered yoga teacher, Ayurvedic Specialist, and publishes under the names Misty Evans & Nyx Halliwell. She's married to her soul mate, has twin sons, and is totally enamored with her three rescue dogs.

Check out her books at www.readmistyevans.com and www.nyxhalliwell.com.

Join her Facebook crystal lovers group, or register for her Crystals 101 online course, Spirit Guides 101 online course, or Crystal Reiki Initiate Course by sending her an email crystalswithmisty@gmail.com .

She sends out a newsletter once a month with all kinds of "woo woo" stuff in it, including energy tips and a crystal of the month. You can subscribe at http://eepurl.com/hfJLiz.

www.ingramcontent.com/pod-product-compliance
Lightning Source LLC
Chambersburg PA
CBHW071959110526
44592CB00012B/1147